A Sharper Silence

Also by Michael Hettich

Books

The Halo of Bees: New and Selected Poems, 1990-2022
The Mica Mine
To Start an Orchard
Bluer and More Vast: Prose Poems
The Frozen Harbor
Systems of Vanishing
The Animals Beyond Us
Like Happiness
Flock and Shadow
Swimmer Dreams
Stationary Wind
A Small Boat

Chapbooks

The Measured Breathing
The Flood (with Carol Todaro)
Measuring the Days
Many Loves
Behind Our Memories
The Point of Touching
Greatest Hits
Singing With My Father
Sleeping With The Lights On
Many Simple Things
Immaculate Bright Rooms
White Birds
Looking Out

Interviews with Poets

And the Poet Said . . .

Collaborative / Handmade Art Books

Home
The Heartland Project
The Ground Beneath Our Feet
Conversation Too (Convo2)

A Sharper Silence

Michael Hettich

Terrapin Books

© 2025 by Michael Hettich
Printed in the United States of America.
All rights reserved.
No part of this book may be reproduced in any manner, except for brief quotations embodied in critical articles or reviews.

Terrapin Books
4 Midvale Avenue
West Caldwell, NJ 07006

www.terrapinbooks.com

ISBN: 978-1-947896-82-6
Library of Congress Control Number: 2025936514

First Edition

Cover art by Claudia Scalise
Beyond the Garden
Gouache on Wood, 2023

for Colleen Ahern-Hettich

1955-2025

in memory

and with abiding love

Contents

The Secret   3

I
First Loves   7
Elegy: Turning Away   9
Intertidal   12
Extinctions   13
Rain   14
Werewolves   15
Certain Secrets   17

II
Lately   21
The Ghost   23
Hunger   24
Unspoken   26
Hatchlings   28
The Dawning   30
The Angels   31
Delicate Bones   32
Palimpsest   34

III
Maybe It's Music   37
Prayer Flags   41
In the Mountains   43
The Distant Music   46
Vase of Silence   48

IV
A Blue Afternoon   53
Yearn   55
Migrations   57
The Perfume   59
Simply by Breathing   61
A Kind of Happiness   62
In the Dream of a Bear   63

The Snag	65
That Glinting	66
A Blessing	68

V

Radiation	71
The Flowers	72
The Lucky Man	73
Angels in the Trees	75
Gratitude	76
Approaching Equinox	77
A Sharper Shadow	78
The Dancers	79
The Field	80

VI

A Strange Sort of Wonder	85
First Light	93
The Window	96
Acknowledgments	99
About the Author	103

When you got tired of walking
you lay down in the grass.
When you got up again, you could see for a moment
   where you'd been,
the grass was slick there, flattened out
into the shape of a body. When you looked back later,
it was as though you'd never been there at all.

                         —Louise Glück, "Pastoral"

The Secret

I'm running through the snow, carrying an injured crow
like a baby in my arms, trying not to fall
in the unplowed road, and hoping he doesn't try
to fly away again, bursting from my arms
to fall into the snow and start flailing, then falling
quiet. I think I'll be able to help him
when I get there, but I don't know how. I don't like
touching wild things, hurt things, but here I am,
and my jacket's all bloody. I'm certain my house
is just up the hill, and I know my wife is waiting there
with coffee and a blazing fire. She laughs when I go out
these frigid early mornings, to wade through the fresh snow
and she laughs when I return. I tell her I love
silence and the cold, after sleeping inside her
warmth as I have done for so many years
I barely remember any other kind of sleeping,
how it would feel now to dream alone,
or how it would stun me to wake up without
her breathing beside me. I tell her these things,
but really I'm searching for something like this darkness
I am carrying now, something I can heal,
or pretend to. And if this animal is dead
by the time I arrive—which I think it will be—
at least I'll have his blood on me, at least I'll have his feathers
to keep on the bookcase and remind me who I am—
and if she's still sleeping by the time I arrive
maybe I'll keep this black bird a secret

after all. I'll bury him in the garden, in the snow,
and let her discover his body, in spring
when the snow melts enough to plant flowers.

I

First Loves

It's the kind of day when you notice your heart
beating, your cellophane lungs crumpling
and opening. You stand still and try to hear
your blood, then wonder which direction it moves,
how far it travels in a day, or in a lifetime.
You listen to the wind cajoling the new leaves
to flutter—and what was the name of that girl
who sat beside you the first day in first grade?
She *fluttered* when you asked her name, then started
to cry. But softly. Your mother had made you
wear a clip-on bow tie, but no one made fun of you,
not even the kid who smelled like day-old
sleep and dirty teeth and made
some other kids cry. His name was Albert.
You went to his house once and woke his mom
who was wheezing and smoking on the couch with the TV
blaring. And now you remember standing
against the wall of the boys' room showing
Albert how far you could pee, when a teacher—
the only male teacher you had then—came in
and pretended to be angry. Albert laughed so hard
he wet his pants. This teacher, you remember now,
was fired from the school later that year,
for being a Communist. This was 1963.
The classrooms had high ceilings, big windows with a long pole
to open from the top; the radiators clanked
and hissed; there were two gyms, one for the girls
and another for the boys—they smelled of wet socks

and polish—so you never got to play bombardment
with that shy girl you'd yearned to comfort, who'd moved
away before Halloween, without
telling anyone, not even your teacher,
whose name was Miss Circle—you remember that seemed
a funny name to have, but a good one.

Elegy: Turning Away

—*Mary Elizabeth Hettich, 1930-2014*

1.

She promises to catch me if I fall, as though
I'm way up high in a tree
and not walking on the sidewalk, holding her hand.
Just look at the leaves she says now, *just look
at the clouds smashing into each other, losing
themselves in each other, turning to rain—*

but she doesn't really *say* this; instead, she says,
*Let's sit on this bench and watch the pigeons
while I smoke a cigarette.* So I listen to the cooing birds
until finally she smiles, stands up and holds out
her hand. We walk to the butcher, then down
to the vegetable market where she tells me to *stay
right here for a minute,* and I breathe the wonderful
smells, watch the flies and the little dog
who runs, yapping, between everyone's feet.

When I lean down to pet him, he licks my mother's
perfume and smell-of-cigarette away.

On the walk home she lets me carry the bag
that smells like lemons and onions and oozes
a little, where I dropped it. Our shadows on the sidewalk
look like one person. As we walk
she promises again to catch me if I fall.

Then we sit down for another cigarette, beneath
huge trees that seem to be whispering to us
as a gentle rain begins—

and she says, *Let's just sit here and see if the trees
will keep us dry. Just sit here beside me.*

So we sit hardly talking and watch the quiet rain.
And when the rain stops, we walk home.

   2.

These many years later, I see her standing
at the open kitchen window
watching the first birds of spring at her feeder,
trying to remember their names, and wishing
she could vanish without
going anywhere, move
out of her body like a breath does, into open air.

She thinks about the distance those small birds have flown
and since I'm still her son, I see her turn away,

I see her turn away now and move through the house
touching her furniture, talking to the pictures
on the walls—not the photographs of family
arranged like a bouquet across her bedroom walls

but the paintings of flowers standing rigid in their vases,
a three-masted schooner moving out to open sea.

3.

Some people can watch other people turn to air
without thinking the air becomes wind too, so it can fly.
I have been like that, capable of watching
as a leaf does, or a window. When she ripped off her skin,
my mother, and lost herself standing there before us
without any skin, and insisted she'd be fine.
When we gathered her shed skin but wouldn't slip it on,
not even over our clothes: It was lumpy
and covered in varicose veins she'd gotten
from the weight of our bodies inside hers, years ago.
When we put her to bed without skin and turned off
the night light and told her to sleep as long
as she wanted to, forever if she wanted to; we would make
breakfast in the morning. When we sat in the kitchen
and looked at each other
and talked about her skin.

Intertidal

Our little house sat at the end of a street
that ran through a marsh which flooded with the tide
and left the city's debris in the cattails
and grasses, where my brother and I

wandered in our rubber boots, clutching sticks
we'd pissed on to give them power, and making
discoveries—a dead swan, long neck curled
around its rotting body, whose feathers stayed white
for days, as the tide hugged it and let go.

We roamed until dusk, pretending we were hunting
water rats and thieves, and sinking down into
the muck, sometimes up to our knees,
having to pull each other free, to walk

reluctantly home as the streetlights came on,
undressing at the front door in the chilly evening air
fragrant with the human smells of wet
lawn and dinner, so different from the funk
of the muck and rotting which thrilled us.

Extinctions

In the back yard we stood in the twilight and watched
thousands of birds flying south.
We wondered if anyone knew who they were,
and we wondered how they knew where to go, whether
we'd ever have any sense of where
we were or where we were going.

In the house, our parents were turning on lights
and walking around with purpose, talking
loudly about things we couldn't understand,
things they *shushed* when we walked into the room.

We could see their shapes through the living room window
as we stood there looking up into the sky
at those thousands and thousands of small lives, flying
somewhere, yelping and singing to each other
as they flew. And when it was too dark to see,
we turned and went inside for dinner.

Rain

—John Hettich, 1956-2015

He is walking by the river, in a spitting rain,
watching the gulls and pigeons, and trying
to remember. He leans on his walker, and looks
across the river to New Jersey. Maybe
he wonders what he's doing out here in the rain—

and then he does remember—or his body does—and he
shuffles on, pushing his walker, stumbling
where the sidewalk is cracked, to a bench, where he sits
and dozes, getting wet, while joggers and dog-walkers
pass, watching him from the sides of their faces,
as though he might be dangerous, or injured,
and they might be called upon to help him.

Soon pigeons have landed; the gulls have circled
and flown off, grousing, toward the bridge,
which hums, as always, with traffic. I can see
his hair now, parted by the gentle rain.
I can see his lightly freckled scalp, and if I lean close,
I think I can hear his breathing.

Werewolves

Sometimes when I walk around the house singing
in my musical-theatre style
of willful jollity, my wife becomes annoyed.
So for a while I shut up
when I hear myself rising to the chorus of "Hello
Dolly," though before long, despite
my best intentions, I forget myself and start
singing that old chestnut I just heard at the supermarket.

In truth, most of what I do or think
is at least half unconscious. I rarely notice
the owl swooping silently across our back yard
to grab the squirrel as I doze and read my book.
Deer step from the woods into the sun
of our garden unnoticed, until I yawn
and they run off in a blur. Even then I'm half-asleep.

When my brother was deaf and living alone
in the apartment he died in, that looked out across
the Hudson to the Palisades, I decided I deserved
to sleep late, after all. I needed to let myself
relax and wake to a big old-style breakfast
instead of flying north to be with him a little while.

He loved watching seagulls and pigeons from his window
and he loved to converse, in his wild disjointed way,
with the neighbors in his building, though they mostly tried
to avoid him. Lonely, he wanted just to keep

talking on and on while they stood patiently
having to pee, or holding bags of groceries.

It was hard to understand what he was saying
about sailboats, stray cats, or waking with his brother
in the middle of a summer night, to walk across the cold grass
and look up at the full moon, hugging his older brother
to keep warm, and talking about werewolves.

Certain Secrets

The names we've never spoken, that define us to ourselves
like the rhythm of a river caught inside a stone
smoothed by that river, as it falls toward the sea.

*

In some other life, I wove grasses and lay down.
In some other life I made a nest and slept,
dreaming like a river, as it slides toward the sea.

*

How many years did we search to find our lives?
How many years do we have before we leave?
The singing of a river as it falls toward the sea

*

is a mind without thoughts, pure being, like the breeze
that wakes in your attic, or underneath your bed
and stirs up the dust, while you're thinking of the sea

*

and hugging your wife, who's dreaming in a language
that doesn't have words yet, and gleams in her eyes
when she wakes in your arms, smelling faintly of the sea

*

and sunlight in the breeze as it moves through the bedroom
then back out the window, like life itself must leave
the body that held it, or a wave far out at sea.

II

Lately

I've caught myself forgetting common words,
blanking on the title of a book I've just read
or the movie we saw last week—even
while I'm lauding its subtle insights,
its moving performances. I've noticed that the more

I worry about these sudden moments of blankness,
these linguistic blind spots, the more often they seem
to visit me. So I think of other things,
or concentrate on synonyms. It's a kind of poetry,
I guess, a lyric of loss. Lately

I've learned that when a cancer patient
is dosed with radiation, she's not filled with light,
though she's hoping to carry the light of her life
a bit longer than she would do otherwise.

The light we can't see kills what will kill her
eventually, or stuns it for a while.

And lately when I sit outside, the squirrels
and chipmunks approach me. The birds seem to think
I'm carrying seed in my hair. They land
in the branches that shade me and mutter to each other,
fly down to hover over my head.

When they realize I'm alive, they flutter off to peck
at the ground; then up into the trees.

It's a bit like being vividly invisible again, like the wind just before it starts to move but holds still, as if waiting.

The Ghost

Reading in the garden, I thought I heard someone
singing in the distance, a beautiful tune
I'd never heard before, so I quieted myself
to listen, as though I might sing along with her

as she walked out of earshot. Then I listened to the breezes
and the light. As a boy I loved to walk home
through the city at dusk as the streetlights came on,

I loved to look into the lit-up rooms
of the houses I passed, to imagine the lives there,
which seemed more *present*, somehow, than my own.

When I reached home, I lingered outside,
watching my family move and talk
to each other as though they were strangers to me,
these people who were usually so familiar
I could hardly see them. I yearned for some sense

of who I was too as I watched my own absence,
soon to be filled, when I walked through the door
as myself, whoever that was then, and disappeared
again into someone
I can't remember now.

Hunger

As I watch a crow glide through the just-budding oaks
    to land in our freshly-turned compost, this crisp
April morning, while I'm clearing the winter
    debris from the path that leads to the creek,

hardly a trickle now, almost silent, as the crow is
    silent, rising with something that looks like
a bread crust or banana peel hanging from its beak—
    no dead mouse, snake or squirrel—big crow,

flying with slow-moving, ballet-dancer wingbeats
    into the sky—an ever-smaller core
of blackness, I wonder for a moment what he sees
    when he sees me, standing out here clearing

twigs and branches, setting them aside
    so nothing will distract us when we step out this evening,
holding glasses of wine, to look up
    at the moon rising and wonder how

it pulls the tides and seasons, even
    the flight of migrating birds—and maybe
we'll wonder a little what the moon
    might see when it sees us, or not *us*

exactly, rather the Earth that is us,
    spinning in its own immense darkness,
pulling the tides in our bodies, whatever
    small oceans we carry and float on. As the darkness

deepens around us, perhaps we'll raise
    a toast to each other, to our blessings, and to the full moon,
as we sip some more wine. Maybe if we stand here
    silently—which I doubt we'll do, being humans

who've drunk a bit by now—perhaps we'll hear an owl,
    way back in the pathless woods, where mushrooms
push up from the leaf-rot into the dark,
    called out of the ground by the same moon

we're out here to celebrate, holding our breath
    to hear that sound again—a distant moan
that reminds us of something we can't name yet recognize—
    the sound of waking without a solid body,

or a body like a tree, swaying and moaning
    in a way that might sound like deep pleasure, at least
to us humans, but is more like the sound of hunger
    that knows how to see through the dark.

Unspoken

Lately I've been discovering wind
in places I'd least expect it—the drawer
where I keep my summer shirts, or the basement
when I go down to bring out the folding summer chairs.

It's a sudden puff or flurry, a tiny explosion
of memory against my face; it makes me
stop breathing for a moment. But where does the wind,
any wind, come from? Is it like language,

emerging from cries and chortles, into
a forest full of paths and grottoes, mushrooms
and berries we could survive on, if
we had to. Luckily we don't have to do that,

at least not yet. And we don't even know
the names of all the insects that live there, or the tiny
orchids that push up through the marl
in the root-crotches down by the creek, and nod

in the wind that sweeps across the ground
or the moss that stays wet all summer, glowing
even on the days when the sun stays hidden,
like the wind in the album of photographs of you

as a young person, waving at the camera to turn
away, look elsewhere, let me comb my hair
and put on nicer clothes, to catch me for the future
in the moment I was beautiful. This wind is like a secret self,

the self that got dressed up, and smiled—but was never
captured. Inside your body—
another kind of wind, full of everything you never did,
all you have forgotten now, glittering like dust motes

or the wings of bees as they land in the blossoms
and poke around, quivering, with what might look like joy.

Hatchlings

I was running through knee-deep surf, trying
not to step on the just-hatched, coin-sized
turtles streaming from the beach.

Out toward the breakers, gulls circled and shrieked,
feasting as the hatchlings swam by.

On the beach, a group of brightly dressed humans
with shovels and nets laughed and clapped.
They didn't seem to notice me running, moving
nowhere, growing more and more exhausted—

and after a while they all turned and walked away
down the beach. So I stopped calling
and decided I might as well lie down, let go
and let the current take me—

I thought about my body, how strong it had once been;
I thought of all the days I'd wasted.

When a squadron of pelicans flew by, swooping down
so beautifully to skim the water's surface,
I felt a surge of gratitude that felt almost
like panic. I noticed one pelican
had a fishing lure caught in the wattle of its massive beak.

It glinted in the sun as the line skimmed along
in the water behind it, as though the huge bird
were pulling something heavy through the waves as it flew,

but it beat its huge wings and glided as though
nothing was wrong, as a dense school of minnows
flashed across my body, casting a shadow
on the sand, and tickling me a little, as they passed.

The Dawning

I looked out the window to see my father,
hands in his pockets, looking up at the dawning sky
as though he were asking it for something. I'd never

seen him look so frail; he seemed a broken man
with nowhere to turn. The stillness of the quiet house
settled around me; my family was still sleeping—
I could almost feel their breathing—and I wanted to go out

and comfort him somehow, tell him it would be
alright—whatever *it* was—though I knew
that was impossible. I was just a boy
and he was my father, who took care of everything.

I could feel the cold glass of the window as I watched him
walk to the curb and lean for the paper,
unfold it there in dawn's light—I've seen
the faithful read sacred texts this way.

I think it was then he sensed I was watching
from above, behind the breath-fogged glass.
His glasses glinted in the early morning light
as he glanced up toward me, then turned to walk inside.

The Angels

As day turned to dusk, we sensed we could feel
the people we'd loved and lost calling
like a breeze that suggests itself but never
actually awakens the trees. She told me
again about the moment she decided to let
our first child go so she could go on
living herself, and I remembered
how once, as a young man, I'd walked by myself
for a day, until I was lost and came
to a boulder and a creek. She remembered yearning
to comfort our baby after we'd scattered
her ashes, and I remembered that the sun
had been warm; the sound of the creek had filled me
with something as different from thought or song
as a dream. She said she still dreamed of Audrey,
our lost child. And then I told her again
that when dusk fell, a clutch of black birds landed.
Even when I stood up and gestured, there
in that unfamiliar landscape, they refused to fly away.
I think they were hungry. But I had nowhere else to go,
so I lay down under stars so sharp
in that darkness they hurt my eyes, even
when my eyes were closed. All night those black birds
stood watching, waiting for something. *Like angels,*
she said then and laughed, though I don't think she was joking.

Delicate Bones

She called to say there was a snake in our bedroom,
nothing to be scared of, just a little guy.
She said I should come home and see it before
it slipped into a closet or under the floorboards.
It looked harmless, she said, and very beautiful.

When she texted pictures, I couldn't help noticing
the bulge halfway down the snake's body, a mouse
or even a chipmunk, and indeed
the snake was a beauty. Then she said it had slipped away
already. I hope it's not hiding in a drawer
or the dirty clothes hamper. I'd told her, I'm sure,
my brother had a boa constrictor as a boy.

Our mother helped him feed it once a month
with laboratory rats she got from the cancer
research center in town.
It took the whole month for the lump in the snake
to move from the front to the back, then out.

By then, just delicate bones, scrubbed clean.

My brother watched that snake while he lay in his bed
recovering from cancer.
He'd been stitched up along the back of his head,
a bit like those test rats. The thread was black

and the stiches looked sloppy, like a badly mended baseball.
I remember how wide the snake opened its mouth
as the dazed rat just seemed to walk in.

Palimpsest

A sapling in a copse of larger trees
at the edge of a mid-winter, snow-dusted field
holds its withered, desiccated leaves
to the thin light and the wind, though those leaves

are skeletons, x-rays of lost hands, their translucent
flesh tattered and fallen away—
the light of stained glass on a cold Sunday morning,
an ancient parchment we squint to read,

whose language we can't know. The tree won't let go—
as though its leaves might never die
if they could be held until spring. And how many
days in your own life will quicken and wake you?

How many days will you hold what you've loved
in yourself and lost while you loved it? Maybe
that's why we walk out on half-frozen lakes
when dusk holds still, before giving way to darkness.

That's how we make ourselves lighter than air
for just a few moments, to make it to the other side.

III

Maybe It's Music

I hardly remember the moments that changed me
most, she says, since I lost myself in them.

And when I emerged, to enter my body
again, it felt like being born
or whatever the trees might feel as they push
out of the ground
and yearn toward the sky

which is nothing, really, except the breath
we've exhaled through eons. And there you are,

my love, sitting in your cave of silence,
born and dying, present and forgotten,
holding your body before me as though

it could ever be solid. I can't touch you where you sing.

*

I tried to think backward when I was most afraid,
to fall through my life
and enter that moment
I became *me*, but I couldn't pull back

deeper than language. Still, somewhere
inside us the world grows wild. Somewhere

inside us the ancient caves are waiting
to be filled again with animals, wild and ravenous,
who will enter the sunlight and eat us where we live.

We sense them approaching each time we blink our eyes.

*

The first time I saw you, he says now, I felt
the trees start burning inside me—while out there

everything remained as it had been before,
glinting and throwing itself toward the light

then curling into sleep, entering dreams
that went on for years, for life. I could show you

dances we do without moving; I could show you
animals leaning out of themselves

into our bodies, animals we can't see
except where we're afraid. Have they come to rescue us

from our surly routines of mind and heart?
Have they come to save us from our automatic lives?

*

But nothing can be saved, after all, except the spaces
between things, moments and objects, thoughts
and blinking eyes. Your heart thumps and patters on

until it doesn't. And if you enter
the cave inside any moment, you might see

paintings on the walls, of animals we've made
extinct, and you might just see darkness, depending
on the light you are carrying inside you.

Or maybe you've come naked, to feel that awesome darkness
and have somehow forgotten your body, after all.

*

Process and design, she says now, is all we are,
like watching the bats flitter back and forth at twilight
then moving off into their darkness, to sleep.

Like watching the deer eat our garden at dawn.
Like scaring them off with a clap and a dance.

Now they watch us from the safety of the woods, big deer

we hardly ever see in broad daylight. And where
do they go when they die? Why don't we find

their bodies in the woods? What grotto holds their bones?
What about the bears, for that matter, or the foxes?

Maybe it's the night birds, that land when we're sleeping
to rip things apart, and carry them away.

What are the names of those night birds, anyway?

And what is that barking, off beyond the trees?
Maybe it's music, not barking after all.

Let's hold each other more still, to listen
until our breaths and heartbeats are everything

and everything is stranger than it's ever been before,
stranger and more beautiful. And always almost gone.

Prayer Flags

After her cancer scan, Colleen and I drive home in silence. It's a beautiful spring day; the early flowers are singing to the bees and butterflies; the tomatoes are starting to blossom. I carry a cup of coffee and a book up to the garden and sit in the sun while she weeds and resonates with what she's just gone through—radiation pulsed through her body—and marvels at the new growth springing up everywhere. She calls up occasionally. She's found a pink lady-slipper orchid back behind the woodpile. She marvels at flowers whose name she doesn't know bursting into blossom by the compost. As she wanders off, weeding her way down the slope, I sit mostly dozing in my own thoughts, dreaming that the prayer flags we've strung between trees up the hill behind me might actually carry healing winds down across our lives. When what sounds like soft snoring startles me awake, I open my eyes to see a bear standing not ten feet away, sniffing the ground as he moves across the garden. I recognize him as the male we've watched since he was a cub, two years ago now. We've watched his mother teach him how to climb trees and we've seen him knock over our garbage. I'm surprised he doesn't see me here, or smell my various human perfumes. I can't smell him either as I sit as still as possible, watching, alert but not afraid, though he could clearly kill me if he wanted to. When the hospital has posted the scan's results this evening, we'll learn whether Colleen's cancer has grown, shrunk, or remained unchanged. Until then we move through a kind of limbo. This bear is just an adolescent, clumsy and hungry. I watch the way his coarse fur gleams in the sun, the way he walks—slightly pigeon-toed—and sniffs at a stump. When I put my book gently down in my lap, he wakes up to me, suddenly alert, as if, like me, he's just been startled to awareness. He snorts and scampers up the hill and into the trees where we've draped those prayer flags. He leaves a faint puff of dust behind him. I get up and wander the garden, leaning to see if he left footprints behind, then call down to Colleen to tell her what I've seen. Soon we'll go inside, open her computer and try to decipher her scans; for now we stand together in amazement under the darkening, late-afternoon sky.

In the Mountains

Summer evenings, we walk the dirt road
to a place where the trees have been cut back

so we can see the mountains
rising in the distance
as if they might stretch themselves, finally, and stand up

to face us, these mountains that have stood since before
there was any such thing as *human*.

Then we walk a bit farther, into the darker woods.

*

Sometimes, before I fall asleep
to the rhythm of her breathing, I yearn to get up
and step outside
to the night creatures singing
such intricate rhythms I might even seem
to disappear inside them—like we seemed to disappear

years ago, high in the Rockies, when,
out of the blue, hail started
to pelt us, buckshot, as the temperature
dropped from July to November. We were suddenly
chattering cold, crouching beneath
a scrawny lodgepole pine, frightened

and laughing. And when the hail stopped—
snowball-sized ice cubes across the open ground.

As they settled and started to melt, they sighed
like a distant breeze, though nothing was blowing.
In fact, the whole landscape was perfectly still.
So we held ourselves still too, and listened.

*

Lost in conversation, we walked across a pond
of slushy ice, past midnight,
at the ashy end of winter.

When we stopped for a moment to look up at the stars,
something in that gesture—the tilting of our heads—

caused the ice to crack. We fell through, first
her, then me, laughing. The pond
was shallow, and the night was silent

so we stood there, up to our knees in the freezing
funky water, and named the constellations
we thought we could identify. Teeth chattering,

we pointed up into the sky, debating what we saw.

*

Sometimes we sing despite ourselves, to feel
the echoing ache in our bodies

while outside a gentle wind carries
the scent of something
that reminds us of something

we loved, a perfume that makes us feel

we could reach out and touch what we'd lost, all those people
and dreams, all those other stories
wandering off, even now, toward evening—

sometimes glancing back, never waving.

The Distant Music

As we drive to town this sunny winter afternoon, we keep passing animals squashed on the highway or torn apart, swollen on the shoulders and in the ditches. The body of a deer is draped across the median. The mountains loom close, dusted a glittering white. Coyote, raccoon. What looks like a skunk and a pet dog. The radio chatters: How do we *portray* ourselves to others? How do we create who we seem to be? Now it cuts to Gaza, Ukraine. On the highway, squashed birds. I think of the red-shouldered hawk we pass on our walk to the meadow. Perched on a wire, she leans to swoop across the field as we approach. By now we've started talking about finding our *authentic selves*, whoever the heck they may be, and I'm wondering again why we never come across dead animals in the woods. The radio host has moved on to climate change. Bears must get killed on the highway too, which is shocking even to imagine, like seeing a mangled person in the grass. I wonder now if they're still winter-napping and if so what they might be dreaming. Spring and summer mornings before we wake up, deer move through our clearing eating the flowers and greens we've planted. We rarely see them, though sometimes I imagine the smell of damp fur and sometimes the garden seems to be quivering a little when I walk out, first thing, with my coffee and the last of my sleep. Humming with something other than the bees, who won't start their work until later. But the spiders have been working. Their webs gleam and buzz with dew and helpless insects. I love to stand still and listen to that music. Sometimes I glimpse the tawny bodies of deer through the trees, watching me, ready to run.

Vase of Silence

> *—This pure silence*
> *that lies beneath all life*
> *seeps into me*
>   —David Vogel (trans. Peter Everwine)

  1.
He picked up his phone, punched some numbers
at random and started to talk to his father,
long disappeared from the planet.

Through the window the trees filled with dusk
then slowly dissolved into darkness.

And the darkness was comforting, somehow, out
beyond the glass. Maybe now
he'd get up, hang up the phone on his father
and walk out into the night.

There were owls in this darkness, silently moving
from tree to tree, big as a child
who wanders out beyond the light
of his family and his house, until he's lost
and sits in the leaves there, waiting.

I was half-asleep, like a river in drought,
a trickle moving
down the mountain toward the sea.

When I woke I was old. No one knew my name.
There were many dark birds in the sky.

   2.
We dozed through the afternoon. When we woke,
there was new singing in the trees.

These are not birds with names, you said
when I started to thumb through our guide book.
These are birds from all the days
we've lived. When we clap our hands,

they'll fly back inside our bodies, though
it will look like they're bursting up into the sky.
You clapped. We waited.

The sun-warmed rocks that circled the field
we were sitting in held even more still
as we gathered ourselves, turned and walked away.

By then we were talking about how it feels to fly
through the darkness, yearning for home.

IV

A Blue Afternoon

        with someone else's mind in my mind, someone
else's memories
coursing through my heart,
        and a whole flock of small birds flying through my body,
high above the clouds, heading south where the land
        has vanished under the rising seas.

    They fly until they fall, and they fall for years:

We were sitting on the terrace with glasses of wine,
        talking in code and watching each other
      through the laughter and silences,

            this fear of letting go
            that defines and keeps us

      from realizing we're falling, though we are falling
   always.

      I remember learning
that somewhere, on the other side of the world,
    there was someone who looked like me, doing
      the things I would do if I lived there, thinking
    thoughts I would think if I spoke his language,
which I didn't. I listened instead

    and heard the world singing to itself as it moved
inside and outside my body, and heard

        someone calling, calling my name
                from a place I could almost remember, like
we almost remember our dreams—or the scent
        of an attic, a basement, a field of fresh cut grass—

Yearn

1.
The saplings we cut at the edge of the trail
push up new saplings we'll cut next year

as the spring wind slips inside our silence,
this dream we find ourselves dreaming together,
as though we've discovered a new world after all.

Maybe we can walk beyond ourselves now.

But that's just the wind, just the wind, stretching
its wings inside silence. There's nowhere else to go
and something in the distance is burning.

2.
This kind of wind never stops, and it never
grows old, though the animals inside it fall away,
the birds flying through it
fall from the sky.

This is the wind inside language when we realize
there are no words, just syntax with nothing
embodied, a creek that's been dammed up completely

but hasn't yet dried: If I could burn
a tattoo of your hands across my body I would do that,
not a decoration but a wound.

3.

If I lay down for a few days, I might become a pond
reflecting what I can't allow inside me—and the rain
would tickle and deepen me, and the shiny little birds
would skim across my body, touching the tips
of their wings just slightly. The ripples they made
would shiver the grasses growing at the shore.

Imagine waking up then, and standing, the waterfall
the body might make
as it walked off through the trees.

Every time you step outside, the animals you know
and the animals you can't know are watching.

Migrations

I can't get my own scent out of my shirts,
he says to his wife in the morning, glancing
out at the colorful birds at the feeder
and sipping his coffee. *Should I try bleach?*

Those ravenous birds have flown thousands of miles,
mostly at night, through the darkness.

Somewhere else a dog swims out through the frigid,
half-frozen harbor looking for its master.
The stars shine bright through swirls of cloud
that show the wind's flailing, so many miles above.

Not a physical fact, the professor
informs his bewildered students, *but
a ghostly system that produces certain
gestures, moods, and states of being:
the workings of power in the ancient world
at work in our own lives, today.*

Another man says he thinks he'll grow a beard
to hide his double chin, if she'll consider
Botox to fill in those wrinkles. Thousands

of migrating birds fly against the windows
of high-rise buildings, to tumble to the sidewalk,
necks broken but hearts still beating.
They quiver and flip-flop on the sidewalk for a while.

When the dog smells his master's cancer, he whimpers
and growls as though that might scare it away.

As he walks home through the evening, whistling
a silly little pop song, the professor stops
mid-tune and starts to hum something more
expressive of his pedigree and style. You never
know when someone might be listening, after all.

Up above the flailing clouds, those tiny songbirds fly.

The Perfume

As he thought about it more, he realized that even
our *numbers* will eventually vanish, dropping
back into infinity. This realization
gave him a strange flush of pleasure at first,
then made him sleepy. Outside the window,

bird shapes were flinging themselves through the trees,
and the wind was scything the grasses. In the kitchen
his wife was puttering, talking to herself
and listening to *All Things Considered,* which is where

he'd heard about the numbers. Soon she would come in
with a glass of wine, or whiskey, and tell him
something about perfume and sweat glands, how
they work together to make a bouquet
like no other scent in the world, unique
to the person who wears it. Then she'd lean down

for a kiss to assure him all would be well,
which he didn't believe for a moment, though he did love
the gentle scent of her perfume, the faint
whiff of her sweat—and he stirred to remember her
laughing to show him her breasts that first time,
shy and yet proud; he remembered how he'd swelled

toward her and opened his body. Soon
the bare trees flailing in the late-winter wind
would ache and swell with what he imagined

was pleasure, and he thought about that pleasure for a while
as he listened to his wife putter in the kitchen
while the radio chattered the news.

Simply by Breathing

I've been breaking things lately, so I can try
to mend them, and learn a new kind of caring—
at least for me—a gentle way to touch
the car-crushed snakes and broken-winged birds

that visit in spring. But really, I can only
wait for them to heal, or die. So I break things
to practice, and then I practice waiting
for the healing. It's a wind I can't hear

unless I hold my breath, another kind of sleep
I wake from, to break things again. No shattered
bones or teeth, no windows or teapots,
just a kind of silence, like the small bone we didn't

realize was scaffolding something inside
until it let go. There's marrow there, even
in such a little bone, so much like a bird's bone,
yearning, even now, to fly. I ask it

to hold still, please, until it's fully healed.
Then I break something else, simply by breathing,
looking out the window, or walking through the woods
searching for a trace of the trail I made

so many years ago now I don't remember where
I thought it might take me. I just kept hacking on.

A Kind of Happiness

It's a relief of sorts to admit I'm a simple
fool when it comes to most practical matters,
balancing the checkbook, let's say, or making
sure my phone is silenced when I'm
sitting in a concert. It's a whole different kind
of relief to hear the wood frogs singing
at the mid-winter thaw, to wonder at the sheer
cacophony of voices, to try to sneak up
to their pond unnoticed and watch them thrash
in their mating. It feels like disappearing
then coming back renewed. Just yesterday, someone
was singing in the distance, down the hill, a woman
whose voice I didn't recognize, though
I recognized the song she was singing, as she
walked off into silence. I sang it all day,
to myself, and it filled me with a kind of happiness,
small but authentic. I harmonized with her
as I moved the stones I had gathered, cradled
like babies in my arms, one after the other,
set them down beside each other,
and drew a new path through the garden.

In the Dream of a Bear

    1.
We barely pause in our conversation
when a red-tailed hawk tumbles through the hemlock,
lands with a thump and a bluster of feathers
then leaps to its feet and flies off.

We don't run to the clearing to watch him disappear
into the sky, or even wonder
what made him fall. We don't scour the ground
where he landed to see what he might have left behind.

We have other things on our minds.

And when the mother bear saunters through our back yard,
followed by two cubs running awkwardly behind her,
then pauses to wait for a third, we watch them
as though we were watching *Wild Kingdom* on TV.

When coyotes wake me in the middle of the night,
these days, I rarely go outside to listen.

Instead I go over what I have to do tomorrow
and try to fall back to sleep. And then
I dream coyotes and hawks, bears
circling our house, peering in.

2.
Yesterday, driving to the store for a bottle
of wine, I hit a squirrel. Of course
I tried to miss it; in fact my swerving
to miss might have caused it to slip
under my tire. I saw it thrashing in my rear-view,

and then I bought my wine. When I drove home, it was gone
or flattened so thoroughly I couldn't see it.

The wine was delicious. I sat on my porch
sipping it like nectar while the last hummingbirds
of the season buzzed at the feeder. Soon
they'll be flying to forests a thousand miles away.

I could hear the highway in the distance, humming
like a faint reminder of something I didn't
want to think about. It was louder than usual.
The music on my phone couldn't cancel it out.

When the breeze shifted slightly, the sound of those cars
blew off into silence and I sat with myself
for a while, wondering what the bears
and coyotes in the woods around our house
might dream, lying there in the darkness.

I imagined myself in the dream of a bear
and wondered what I'd look like there.

Somehow this thought made me happy.

The Snag

The huge red oak, long dead, by the creek
    has been leaning against a smaller living tree
for years, moaning when the wind cajoles it

even slightly—like an owl in the night woods
    heard at a distance, a sound we stand still for,
my wife and I, to feel our own breathing.

A few times I've tried to push it from the living tree's
    branches, but it won't budge. It's been leaning
so long its bark's worn away, smooth wood

gone black. It could kill with the weight of its falling,
    and it will fall, of course, someday when no one's
standing there to see it. She said she wondered

what it felt like to be born, to move from that darkness
    in a sudden burst of energy and breathing; she told me
she sometimes felt empty of herself, like a ghost.

We were sitting outside to watch the summer light
    as it faded, listening to a barred owl moan
in the distance and waiting for something whose name

we didn't know, something like an animal approaching
    in a language we'd forgotten, and all we could do now
was open our arms, and wait for it to come.

That Glinting

Then someone discovered certain winds could turn inward,
blow around where nothing has happened, no one
has yet been born--like touching your love
who falls away to dust, then blows into another
language we've been speaking all the time without knowing
it's a prayer, like the grasses might sing, of perfect

being: I want to make sure I'm as real
as water under water
that's deeper than light,
water at the bottom of the world beyond darkness,
water under such pressure it might

explode like wind if it could be brought
to the surface: wind from some ancient time

or just another present moment, glinting in the window
of an old woman's kitchen. She is singing as she pulls
the curtains to soften that glinting, turns back
to her cats who are purring
in response to her song,

which is tuneless, like a wounded animal, out
in the woods we are passing now, moving toward night

as the radio chatters incomprehensibly
though we grew up with the songs it's playing, so many

years ago we hardly remember who we were then,
though we do remember the words to those songs;

it's as though we were falling, falling through our bodies
toward a puddle-sized swimming pool, preparing ourselves
to slip into the water like dancers, or as though

we could remember the feeling of slipping
through our mother's body into this bright world,

carried by her screams of pain and strangled joy,
then screaming ourselves, pink and helpless, knowing

absolutely nothing
about anything at all.

A Blessing

Next day, the solstice, we got up at dawn
and drove to Chaco, arriving just before
the real heat set in. We spent the day
exploring the ruins, feeling the wide-open
landscape, and looking for shade. That evening

we met a naked-eyed astronomer, a Native
American man, who told us the names
of the stars and constellations, for hours, and would have
talked through the night if we hadn't been growing
too sleepy to listen. His song braided myths

and science, stories from Europe, Asia,
Africa, and Native America. He was teeming
with enthusiasm and generosity,
pointing to the sky as he adjusted his telescope
so we could look up at what amazed him, while he

told us something new. Next morning, at dawn,
at the sacred *kiva* where we'd gathered to watch
the sun shoot precisely through a niche in the wall,
as it has done for a thousand years,
this man was praying quietly, sitting perfectly still.

We thanked him again, without saying anything.
That evening we drove on, east to Santa Fe.

V

Radiation

A man and a woman, not old but deeply
tired, walk down a basement hallway,
holding each other with breath and being,
both of them frightened, the woman in pain,
walking erect, as the nurse opens
a door, ushers them in, and asks
if they might need a blanket or a glass
of water—anything at all. She smiles
and begins to ask questions. As she writes,
she stops to look into the woman's eyes.
Then she leans out and gently touches the woman
on the arm, pats it softly, and smiles.
She looks right into this frightened woman's
face, whispers *be well*, and smiles
again, as the doctor walks in, nods
to them all, sits down, and begins to explain,
slowly, so they fully understand
what is to come, and how it will change things
in the short run and the long. He too
smiles and nods as they thank him, turns
and leads them back into the hall, and out
into the huge bright world, where they stand
blinking and dazed for a moment. Then
they get in their car and drive home.

The Flowers

That first year in the tropics, we'd swim out farther
than we dared—though we did it—until we reached the sandbar
almost out of sight of land, where the gently lapping water
was so shallow we could sit down and let its gentle rocking
soothe us until we were drowsy—not tired
exactly but half-dreaming, gazing at the vastly deeper
water beyond us and the darker currents running there.

We'd wade along that sandy ridge watching minnows scatter
and the bigger fish flash like flint and disappear.
Pelicans, anhinga, and black skimmers let us come close—

We'd moved from the gray north; our bones still ached with cold.

That ocean smelled like flowers whose names we hadn't learned yet,
and it was warm enough for us to take off our suits
and sing like children, and talk like children back and forth,
not baby-talk but a kind of innocence—

then we'd push off to swim in, across the calm but teeming water
back to the city with its dancing and its rage
and its many kinds of flowers whose names we also didn't know,
though we were determined to learn them.

The Lucky Man

As we walk to the waterfall this sunny summer afternoon, she reminds me that her father built her childhood home with her grandfather, brick by brick. That's why there were windows in some of the closets, she says: he learned by doing. *That's why my mother kept rolls of dollar bills in the pockets of her winter jackets. Just in case.* The house was solid but awkward and cramped; the stairs were as steep as a ladder and the kitchen was smaller than a rich person's bathroom. There were five children in the family.

While we sit beside the river to eat lunch, she talks about tying flies with her father, down in that cluttered unfinished basement while the snow fell outside to dim the windows and the rest of the family ate popcorn in the living room with the TV blaring. She could hear its muffled voices as she sat next to her dad, whose breath smelled like coffee and whose forearms were pink and almost hairless. She listened to his breathing as he showed her how to cut and tie.

Grayhackle Special; Lefty's Deceiver; Pheasant Tail Nymph . . .

Her mother had taught her how to sew her own clothes. When we first met, she made my shirts and pants, beautiful garments I was reluctant to wear in case I spilled something, or ripped them.

The day after we met, we hiked up into the mountains and she caught two trout with flies she'd tied herself, then gutted the fish in one gesture and cooked them with garlic. We slept with our heads poked outside the tent, so we could look up at the stars.

Angels in the Trees

My wife drapes her drying dresses across
the mountain laurel branches; she forgets them
all night, and in the morning, walking out,

she thinks for a moment she sees a choir
of angels standing at the edge of the woods,
watching her. But it's only her dresses,
full of dew, and smelling clean as snow.

Her most beautiful dress hangs deeper in the woods,
higher in the branches. We wonder how it got there

as I prop a ladder inside the flurry
of twigs and leaves, climb up and carefully
carry it down. It's covered now

in tiny inch worms, so we hang it in the sun
and watch them slip to the ground on their strands
of glinting filament. Then she puts it on,

this dress I bought her when we were still almost
children. She'd stopped and gasped when she saw it
in the shop window. It fit perfectly then—

but she looks even more beautiful now
all these years later, as she walks around the garden
smiling at the new flowers, barefoot in the sun.

Gratitude

Night emerges from the morning woods
        to move across the tall grass toward us, sighing
                faintly in the fresh light, as though it were confused.

        We call to it gently, like we might call a stray dog,
                or someone's lost pet, holding ourselves
        ready to pull back if it threatens to hurt us.

But this darkness is neither starving nor dangerous,
        so we let it come close enough to pet, until
somehow it enters our bodies, like language

        enters a child, to make that child real
                to itself. It's a language we've spent most of our lives
        learning to speak, though we're still not able

to say what we mean exactly: *I love you*
        in words that capture the rivers and streams,
                the huge flocks of birds, the silences,

                and the stunning losses that resonate still
        at the core of our deepest contentment, all
                the nights we've hugged in sleep, dreaming

        worlds we'll forget as we wake, again,
into a blessedly ordinary day,
        one of many hundreds, hardly noticed as it passes.

Approaching Equinox

These trees hold still, as if they were expecting
their birds to arrive, waiting for the weight
of those famished bodies to land and sing
I am starving to the grasses and leaves.

Yesterday we got lost when the deer trail
we'd been following petered out halfway up the mountain
and we tried another fainter trail which petered out too.

Sometimes if you lie down and pretend to go to sleep,
animals you'd never meet otherwise will come out
and watch you, sniffing the air to discover
what you've been eating
and how long you'll likely live.

In the morning we collect the bodies
of the sparrows who have flown against our windows.
We bury them in a shoebox beside the compost pile
and try to imagine the wide sky they flew through
above the rain clouds, mostly at night,

these fierce little creatures, so comely and light
we might even think they weighed nothing.

A Sharper Shadow

Sometimes when we sit without talking for a while,
the light seems to fall through the trees with a different
sense of itself. I feel something of the *tenuous*,
even in our silence, as though we were counting
our breaths, preparing ourselves to let go
of each other, maybe sooner than we know.

This ache feels more deeply interfused than love,
though of course it is love too. It casts a sharper shadow
than love, even love that lasts a lifetime.
It's like a map of being, deeply etched wood grain,

or the way snow falls into an unmown field
through the stillness of an afternoon: Something in that light
moves into the shape of things and changes their contours
as dusk rises to meet the sky—

and the snow falls all night, to glow in the morning,
trackless but shadowed by the gently blowing grasses
which lean down, sometimes, to draw circles in the powder
and sometimes stand still, as if waiting.

The Dancers

We were climbing Glass Mountain on a summer afternoon,
stopping to look through the trees at the farms
and forest beyond, unscarred, as far
as we could see from the distance of the mountain,

which opened at the summit to a sloping granite landscape,
gentle and dramatic at once, where the ice
in winter forms a sheet—like glass—
but was dry now, and warm in the sun.

We sat and marveled at the pines that grew there,
somehow, out of a seam in the granite.
We wondered how old they might be.
They gestured like ancient bonsai, twisted
like dancers caught mid-stride.

Then she told me she loved dancing
almost beyond any other pleasure.
She talked about the men she'd danced with before
we'd met—not jumping around in a drunken
sort of stupor, but dancing with a give-and-take,

dancing with the mind as well as the body.
I don't think we've ever done that, however hard we've tried.

The Field

I love to kiss you, she says now, when you seem
to be only half-sleeping. I love to wonder
what you're thinking, lying beside me,
just before you fall away. I wonder if our dreaming
makes a halo around us, a field of humming energy
only the sharpest ears can discern—

a voice that calls from across a wide river,
like the river we stood beside yesterday, humming
together at the frequency we've come to call our love.

As we stood looking out, hardly breathing,
and watched the water roll on toward the ocean
half a continent away, I felt a rush of gratitude
that shivered and clarified, another kind of singing,
as my body prepares itself for yet another series
of invasions: radiation, promised not to harm
but what it's meant to kill. I'll lie still, shot full

of a light that sees secrets we can't know we're keeping
and kills them where they grow. Just handle me with care
I'll ask the machines as they plumb and light my body,
as if they could feel anything. But it's a kind of prayer,

and what else can I do? I love to wake beside you
and listen to your breathing, and breathe along with you,
cocooned in the night creatures' silence. Yesterday,
returning from that river through a field of tall grass,

we could have lain down to disappear a while,
looked up at the sky moving blue above us,

and waited for dusk. But we didn't need to vanish yet,
even if just briefly. We were still too full of light.

VI

A Strange Sort of Wonder

—for Shannon and Joel Bruggen

When the storm had passed, a stillness filled the day
with a quiet deeper than silence—

like the sound of blood when we're sleeping, or dreams
when we wake. Then it moved off into the trees

like an echo of an even deeper silence,

as many of the big trees, oaks mostly, sighed
and let themselves fall
into each other's arms

like lovers—to lie across roads, cars
and houses, while the rivers kept swelling, taking

bridges and businesses, turning roads into rapids
that swept cars and families away. One day

the world was familiar; the next it was utterly
changed. Or just gone. And that silence persisted

in the ways we moved
and talked to each other,
in the language we used with ourselves when we were

alone. The nights were so dark beyond
the houses, up in the broken woods
and down in the folds and hollows of the mountains,

out on the swept-away farms.

*

We'd lost power and water; the roads were washed out.

Dozens of big trees had fallen near our house,
but our house itself was undamaged.

We felt lucky, of course, but we couldn't get out
except on foot. We knew we couldn't do that—

and we knew we'd soon have to. Colleen was weak
from chemo. She'd had a pleura drain installed
a few days before, so I could drain her lungs
when they filled with liquid. It was an intimate,

delicate, potentially disastrous procedure
that required all tools, especially hands,
to be germ-free—a challenge, to say the least,
without clean water.

We had a creek down the hill and some five-gallon jugs.
Hand sanitizer. We cooked on the grill.

Evenings we sat out, talked softly, listened
to the night creatures sing, and marveled at how quickly
so much we had taken for granted, and loved
without thinking about it, was gone.

*

After a few days, our daughter and her husband
bushwhacked to our house
and convinced us to try

to get out while we could, before the last bridges
collapsed completely. Casey helped me

navigate the torn-up road and the crumbling

bridge out of town, to Charlotte, then on
to Winston-Salem, where we stayed with friends

we'd known only slightly
before the storm.

And though we stayed for a month, eating
their food, drinking their wine, and sleeping
in their best bedroom, they never made us feel

anything but welcome.

*

Sometimes, after sleeping nearly
the whole day, she woke and told me dream
after dream, one leading vividly into
another, all of them uniquely surprising

and wild. Then she said she wanted
to sleep again, since sleep allowed her
to feel her body as though her body

were still taut and skittish, to live in that vividness
again, at least for a while. *Thank you,*

she said when I turned up the heat, or covered
her legs in the colorful blanket she loved.
Thank you for cooking such a wonderful-smelling
dinner I can't eat: the smell of your cooking

is pleasure enough. Or almost. Or really,
hardly at all, though it's better than nothing.

Then she was breathing deeply again,

so I sat in the bedroom, eating and breathing
beside her. As evening darkened the lawn
beyond the big picture window, deer
emerged from the woods, almost impossible
to see in the gathering darkness
but there nonetheless, like another sort of dream.

I watched until they'd faded completely,
then I got up, went out, walked across the lawn
and lay down in the chilly, dew-drenched grass
as though I might understand something that way
or feel something new. But cold is just cold—

so I went back into the house, took off
my clothes, and slipped into bed beside her.

I warmed myself beside her all night while we slept.

*

Some nights I seemed to be walking with a candle
through a maze of dark rooms, looking for something
I wasn't even sure of, maybe a window

or a door. The rooms were cluttered; there was furniture
pushed up against the walls, and the air smelled like fallen
leaves. My feet made the whispering *swoosh*
of walking through the woods in autumn, though of course
there were no trees here. I thought I saw a light,
like another candle, down a hall, then doubted
myself. But still, I kept walking.

Other nights I was sitting in an easy chair reading,
or pretending to. Really, I was dreaming words
into stories as I looked down into my bare hands,
my dear hands, I thought, which had served me so well
for so many years. I wanted to reach out
and touch her, breathing beside me, but for some reason
I was afraid to move, as though by moving
I might truly feel what we'd lost. The darkness

lay like an animal across our bodies,
warm and purring and wild.

*

The next morning, when we arrived at the hospital
for Colleen's chemo, the receptionist asked us
how we'd fared in Helene,

so we told her in detail. We took a certain
pleasure in recounting the challenges of navigating
the washed-out mountain roads, the thrill
of driving across a half-collapsed bridge,
the frustrations of trying to syphon gas
from a tree-smashed car, to fill our own
so we wouldn't run dry on the highway.

We left out the fear, the pain, and the exhaustion.
Without meaning to do so, we made what had happened
sound almost like an adventure.

When we finally asked the same question of her,
she smiled and told us—matter-of-factly—
she'd lost everything, or *almost* everything,
when her apartment flooded. It had all washed away.

She'd managed to pack her car with her most
precious possessions—heirlooms and photos
of her family. Then her car had been stolen—
so now she *really* had nothing. *I'm okay,*

she said then and looked straight up into Colleen's eyes.
In fact, she said, *I feel lucky.*

*

Sometimes she wakes me in the middle of the night
because she can't sleep for the pain, so I get up

and rub her back. And though I don't think
it gives her much relief, or helps with the fear,

it lets her relax into sleep. When she's finally
peaceful, I lie beside her, on the narrow

sliver of bed, in the middle of the night,
and I feel an almost overwhelming gratitude

I've never felt before, a love I'm just learning
to live inside of, more difficult than anything

I've known, darker but also more potent,
and filled with a strange kind of wonder

that frightens me beyond my little self. *And then I'm gone.*

*

Will we leave any trace when we vanish from our bodies,
the way the downed trees
leave their trace across the land,

an absence that beckons new life from the ground?

Will something like our breath continue to move
through grasses and bushes and ferns, to ripple

the pond we love, that holds itself tighter
each day, as winter approaches?

Of course not, though it's somehow reassuring
to consider, an idea that gives solace,
if only briefly. Already the land
is healing, the sun warms the ground in different
places now, and the breeze moves differently.

In spring, new saplings and flowers—.

*

Many years ago, high in the Rockies,
we crossed a mountain river in June,
fast moving and freezing with snowmelt. We took off

our pants and held them above our heads
as we waded waist-deep, yelping, then jumping
with joy and amazement—we'd made it across!

So we walked a bit farther, to a meadow teeming
with spring wildflowers
nodding in the morning sun.

At the edge of that field there were drifts of snow
gleaming as they melted. *This is where we'll live*

from now on, together, she said to me then.
I felt what she meant, and agreed.

First Light

1.
As I walk to the kitchen in the pre-dawn light,
I glance out the window: dark forms etched in darkness

out by the compost, just far enough away
I can't tell at first if they're really *there*.

I lean closer, squinting. Shapes tumble and lie still,
wrestling and eating the scraps I dumped last night:

a family of bears—momma and three almost
full-grown cubs. So I step out, half-dressed

and still half-asleep. There's a garden wall between us
and I'm hardly a threat, skinny old half-naked

human that I am. I walk out into the chilly dawn
holding my breath, doing my best

to disappear. But of course they sense me anyway,
right away, and bound off through the trees

with what looks like joy, if joy is that feeling
of throwing oneself into the moment without thinking,

just losing yourself for a while. Last night

before we turned off the light, I rubbed
Colleen's shoulders and back with a lotion

that sometimes relieves her pain. As I rubbed
and sang softly, mostly to myself,

I could feel how her delicate bones worked to hold her
together, how fragile that scaffolding is,

and I tried to work deeper—to give her some relief,
which is almost impossible now.

All day I'd been moving branches and stones
the big storm scattered, soothing the wounds
the fallen trees left, as though I could make things
beautiful again with my human puttering.

The beauty I yearn for will come back despite me.
I pull another root ball off the path and feel

my wife's small bones beneath my fingers.

   2.
The little creek we love, that runs along the edge
of our property, has vanished under rubble,

though farther down the mountain it emerges again,
singing with the same voice it had before the storm,

at least to my ears, though maybe I'm not listening
carefully enough, since the path it sings

has changed so dramatically, and all the little creatures—
salamanders, mud-puppies, and the nameless ones too—

were buried in the landslide.

Most likely my ears just aren't built to hear
the different voices in the water as it falls

from darkness into daylight, falls toward the bigger creeks
and rivers, on into the manmade lakes

of this region, then on toward the ocean, the pulse
of tides more ancient than mountains or rivers

or even life itself as we know it, though somehow
it sings, it sings in us still.

The Window

The silence was suddenly tuned to a different
key, she says; it felt hollow, and it echoed

like the hush after a rush-hour train
that doesn't stop at the station. *Look at me—*

the secret rooms we live in, the windows
we open when there's nothing left
to see. And now

I feel as though no one has known me, ever.
That kind of silence. *Touch me.* Once,

while I slept, I turned transparent.
The moon shone through my body, waxing
and waning,

pulling tides and long migrations,
turning me wild. No one knows my name

except you, and you're sailing off into the distance,
waving for help, or goodbye.

Acknowledgments

Thanks to the editors of the following journals in which many of these poems first appeared, often in slightly different form.

Bacana Poetry Review: "Elegy: Turning Away"

Blueline: "The Snag"

Bracken: "The Ghosts"

Escape into Life: "Gratitude," "The Perfume," and "Turning Away" (first section)

Evening Street Review: "The Lucky Man"

Hamilton Stone Review: "The Distant Music," "A Kind of Happiness," and "Unspoken"

Live Encounters Poetry: "Radiation" and "Werewolves"

Midwest Quarterly: "Migrations" and "The Secret"

North Carolina Bards: "A Blessing" and "Hunger"

One Art: "The Flowers"

Painted Bride Quarterly: "First Loves"

The Power of the Pause: "Palimpsest" and "A Sharper Shadow"

Real South/West: "Lately"

Rockvale Review: "In the Mountains"

Slant: "The Dawning," "Delicate Bones," "Simply by Breathing," "Slip Away," and "Yearn"

Split Rock Review: "Angels in the Trees" and "Approaching Equinox"

Terrain: "A Blue Afternoon," "Extinctions," and "That Glinting"

Two Hawks Quarterly: "The Snag"

Under a Warm Green Linden: "First Light" and "Maybe It's Music"

Vilas Avenue: "Intertidal"

Willow Springs: "The Dancers," "First Loves," and "Prayer Flags"

Sections from "A Strange Sort of Wonder" (titled "A Quiet Deeper than Silence") appeared in an anthology entitled *Unnatural Disasters in Appalachia: Poets Respond to Devastating Floods,* ed. Hilda Downer (Redhawk Publications, 2025).

"First Loves" and "Werewolves" were reprinted in *Chiron Review.*

"The Angels" was featured by the *Academy of American Poets, Poem-a-Day on January 3, 2025.*

Thank you to my family: Matthew Hettich, Caitlin Hettich, Casey Sharpe, Emmanuelle John, Owen Sharpe, and Leo Sharpe.

Thank you to Jesse Millner for reading early drafts of many of these poems.

Thank you Mitchell Kaplan, Heidi Lellelid, Campbell McGrath, Claudia Scalise, Kevin Morgan Watson, Elizabeth Jacobson, David Kaufman, Tom Virgin, Karen Osborne, Joel Bruggen, Shannon Bruggen, Ken Kelly, Kitty Kelly, Bill Schulz, Michael Blanchard, Anouschka Rachelson, Carolina Hospital, and Kimberly Standiford.

Thank you Diane Lockward.

Thank you to all who loved Colleen.

About the Author

Michael Hettich has published more than a dozen books of poetry, most recently *The Halo of Bees: New and Selected Poems, 1990-2022* which won the 2024 Brockman-Campbell Book Award from the North Carolina Poetry Society. His other honors include several Individual Artist Fellowships from the Florida Division of Cultural Affairs, The Tampa Review Prize in Poetry, the David Martinson / Meadowhawk Prize, a Florida Book Award, the Lena M. Shull Book Award from the North Carolina Poetry Society, and the inaugural Hudson-Fowler Prize from *Slant* magazine at the University of Central Arkansas. His poetry, essays, and reviews have appeared in many journals and anthologies. He holds a Ph.D. in literature and taught for many years at Miami Dade College. He lives in Black Mountain, North Carolina.

www.ingramcontent.com/pod-product-compliance
Lightning Source LLC
Chambersburg PA
CBHW060533080526
44586CB00012B/719